ilovemyjobnotebooks.link/bulk-offers

Copyright © 2025 by I Love My Job Notebooks

All rights reserved. No part of this book may be reproduced without written permission of the copyright owner, except for the use of limited quotations for the purpose of book reviews.

This Journal is Sponsored by

Paramount Digital Publishing, LLC

We believe work should be more than survival — it should be purposeful, energising, and scalable.

That's why **Paramount Digital Publishing, LLC** proudly supports *I Love My Job Notebooks* — a space for reflection, growth, and skilful living for today's professionals.

🚀 **Want to do more with less?**

AI Automation for Busy Founders & Teams

✓ 80% fewer support headaches
✓ 24/7 lead-gen on autopilot
✓ We manage the tech — you focus on growth

Book Your Free AI Discovery Call

ilovemyjobnotebooks.link/dmm

Scan below to explore smarter systems that free up your time, reduce overwhelm, and help you scale without burning out.

Forever grateful to you

This notebook belongs to:

____

Gifted by:

____

A little space to reflect, reset, and reconnect with what matters most.

■ *What story are you telling yourself today?*

■ *List three wins, even if they're tiny. Do it now.*

■ *Invisible effort often builds visible results later.*

■ *Multitasking kills momentum. Try one thing at a time.*

■ *What would change if you gave yourself the benefit of the doubt?*

Energy flows where clarity goes. Start with what matters most.

■ *Boundaries are bridges, not walls.*

■ *People won't always remember your skills, but they'll remember how you made them feel.*

■ *A 5-minute break can unlock your next hour of flow.*

■ *What if today's delay is training for tomorrow's breakthrough?*

■ *You don't have to earn rest. You just need to honour it.*

■ You're already worthy. Now act like it.

■ *You carry value even on your low-energy days.*

■ *Your value isn't in how much you do. It's in how much you align.*

■ *Send a kind message to a colleague — no context needed.*

■ *Progress is still progress, even if no one sees it.*

■ *Protect your peak energy hours like gold.*

■ *Believe you can handle it — even before you know how.*

■ *Respect is felt, not spoken. Let your presence do the work.*

■ *Speak to yourself like you would someone you care about.*

■ *Let go of perfection. Aim for progress today.*

■ *You're not meant to do it all. You're meant to do what matters.*

■ Check in: Are you moving with intention or momentum?

■ *Today is not a test. It's a chance.*

■ *Energy management beats time management every time.*

■ *Kindness to yourself is not optional. It's foundational.*

■ *Say no without explaining. Your worth doesn't need proof.*

■ Discomfort is data. Listen, then respond.

■ *Growth looks like small quiet steps repeated.*

■ *You don't need to fix everything today.*

■ *Today's version of you is already enough.*

■ *Try asking: "What do I need right now?"*

■ *Self-trust is built one promise kept.*

■ *Start before you feel ready. Confidence follows action.*

Doubt shows up before big moves. Expect it, don't obey it.

■ *You're allowed to outgrow the old version of you.*

■ *Show up gently. That's still showing up.*

■ *Some days are for maintaining, not conquering.*

■ *You're not lazy. You're likely overloaded.*

■ *Regret less. Reflect more.*

■ *Tiny pivots shape big outcomes.*

■ Embrace effort, not just results.

■ *Create quiet moments between tasks today.*

■ *Notice your tone when you talk to yourself.*

■ *Choose one priority — and protect it.*

■ *"No" is a complete sentence.*

■ *Ask yourself better questions, not harsher ones.*

■ *Your body often knows before your mind catches up.*

■ *Pause before reply — not everything needs a response.*

■ *You're not too much. You may be in the wrong room.*

■ *Seek clarity, not certainty.*

■ *Don't outsource your peace to other people.*

■ *You can disappoint others and still be in integrity.*

■ *Show up as the person you're becoming — not who you've been.*

■ *Today is a good day to be kind to yourself.*

■ You don't need more time. You need more alignment.

■ *Protect your "yes" by using "no" wisely.*

■ *If you're tired, rest. Not quit.*

■ *Find the smallest possible win — and go do that.*

■ *You're allowed to say "I don't know."*

■ *"Done" is better than "perfect" every time.*

■ *Decide what you're not doing today.*

■ *Celebrate effort — not just outcomes.*

■ *You're not meant to be available 24/7.*

Your space to turn ideas into action — one small step at a time.

SKILLFUL LIVING COMPANION WORKBOOK

This workbook is designed to work with any Skillful Living Guide. Whether you're diving into mindfulness, health, productivity, or relationships — these pages will help you turn inspiration into action.

Think of it as your personal coach in notebook form: here to help you track habits, reflect on lessons, and make changes that stick.

Use this workbook to:

- Capture "aha!" moments before they vanish.
- Break down big ideas into doable daily steps.
- Stay accountable — even on the messy days.

ACCESS YOUR GUIDE

Unlock free practical exercises, tools, and challenges.

ilovemyjobnotebooks.link/skillfulliving

1. KICKSTART

Let's start with your why — because vague goals lead to vague results.

1 **Which guide are you using today?**

(e.g., Mindful Walking, Protein-First Shop, Digital Declutter)

2 **What's your BIG goal from this guide?**

(e.g., "Walk every day without making it a chore")

3 **Why does this goal matter to you right now?**

(e.g., "I feel burnt out and want a daily reset")

Write the top 3-5 things you learned from the guide. Use your own words so they stick.

(e.g., "Plan protein first, carbs second when shopping")

(e.g., "Walk slow enough to actually notice my surroundings")

1 ____

____

____

2 ____

____

____

3 ____

____

____

4 ____

____

____

5 ____

____

____

3. MY PERSONAL PLAN

Get specific — "I'll eat better" isn't a plan, it's a wish.

This week I will:

(e.g., "Cook chilli on Sunday for 3 dinners")

1 ____

2 ____

3 ____

4 ____

5 ____

6 ____

I will do them because:

- (e.g., "I want to feel more energised and less stressed at work")

____

____

____

____

____

Life happens — be ready for it.

Things that might get in the way:

(e.g., "Rainy weather", "Late nights", "Colleagues bringing cake")

1
2
3
4
5

How I'll handle them:

(e.g., "Keep an umbrella by the door", "Meal prep before busy days")

1
2
3
4
5

Plan it like you mean it — then tick it off like a boss.

Day	Planned Action(s)	Done?
Monday		☐
Tuesday		☐
Wednesday		☐
Thursday		☐
Friday		☐
Saturday		☐
Sunday		☐

5. WEEKLY PLANNER

Plan it like you mean it — then tick it off like a boss.

Day	Planned Action(s)	Done?
Monday		☐
Tuesday		☐
Wednesday		☐
Thursday		☐
Friday		☐
Saturday		☐
Sunday		☐

Plan it like you mean it — then tick it off like a boss.

Day	Planned Action(s)	Done?
Monday		☐
Tuesday		☐
Wednesday		☐
Thursday		☐
Friday		☐
Saturday		☐
Sunday		☐

Celebrate the numbers and the feels.

Date	Result / Number / Outcome	Mood / Energy
(e.g., "Monday –	8,000 steps –	Mood: 8/10")

Celebrate the numbers and the feels.

Date	Result / Number / Outcome	Mood / Energy
(e.g., "Monday –	8,000 steps –	Mood: 8/10")

7. REFLECTION

Think of this as a quick debrief with yourself.

What worked well this week?

(e.g., "Prepping lunches in advance made mornings easy")

1 ____

2 ____

3 ____

What didn't work?

(e.g., "Tried evening workouts but kept skipping them")

1 ____

2 ____

3 ____

What will I change for next week?

(e.g., "Switch workouts to mornings before work")

1 ____

2 ____

3 ____

Think of this as a quick debrief with yourself.

What worked well this week?

(e.g., "Prepping lunches in advance made mornings easy")

1 ____

2 ____

3 ____

What didn't work?

(e.g., "Tried evening workouts but kept skipping them")

1 ____

2 ____

3 ____

What will I change for next week?

(e.g., "Switch workouts to mornings before work")

1 ____

2 ____

3 ____

Think of this as a quick debrief with yourself.

What worked well this week?

(e.g., "Prepping lunches in advance made mornings easy")

1
2
3

What didn't work?

(e.g., "Tried evening workouts but kept skipping them")

1
2
3

What will I change for next week?

(e.g., "Switch workouts to mornings before work")

1
2
3

Because sometimes you win in ways you didn't expect.

Unexpected benefits:

(e.g., "Spent less money on takeaway", "Slept better", "Met a neighbour on my walk")

9. MOVING FORWARD

Lock in your biggest win from this guide.

If I could keep only ONE habit from this guide, it would be:

(e.g., "Walking every day without checking my phone")

♥ **One weekly tip to simplify eating, planning and living**

Struggling to eat well without overthinking it?

Join the Skillful Living Newsletter and get your free **Zero-Stress Meals Guide** — **5 ADHD-friendly**, one-bowl meals ready in 15 minutes.

Get recipes + life tips weekly — scan for your first freebie

ilovemyjobnotebooks.link/zerostress

💼 Loved using this book?

 Grab another for a teammate or work friend at

ilovemyjobnotebooks.link/chat

💡 For bulk/team orders, visit:

ilovemyjobnotebooks.link/bulk-offers

Printed in Dunstable, United Kingdom